Empires in the Middle Ages

The Crusades

Edited by
Carolyn DeCarlo

Britannica Educational Publishing
in association with
ROSEN
Educational Services

Published in 2018 by Britannica Educational Publishing (a trademark of Encyclopædia Britannica, Inc.) in association with The Rosen Publishing Group, Inc. 29 East 21st Street, New York, NY 10010

Distributed exclusively by Rosen Publishing.
To see additional Britannica Educational Publishing titles, go to rosenpublishing.com.

First Edition

Britannica Educational Publishing
J.E. Luebering: Executive Director, Core Editorial
Andrea R. Field: Managing Editor, Compton's by Britannica

Rosen Publishing
Carolyn DeCarlo: Editor
Nelson Sá: Art Director
Brian Garvey: Designer
Cindy Reiman: Photography Manager
Nicole Baker: Photo Researcher

Library of Congress Cataloging-in-Publication Data

Names: DeCarlo, Carolyn, editor.
Title: The Crusades / edited by Carolyn DeCarlo.
Description: New York : Britannica Educational Publishing in Association with Rosen Educational Services, 2018. | Series: Empires in the Middle Ages | Includes bibliographical references and index. | Audience: Grades 5–8.
Identifiers: LCCN 2017014865| ISBN 9781680487817 (library bound : alk. paper) | ISBN 9781680488609 (pbk. : alk. paper) | ISBN 9781680488708 (6 pack : alk. paper)
Subjects: LCSH: Crusades—Juvenile literature.
Classification: LCC D157 .C7637 2018 | DDC 909.07—dc23
LC record available at https://lccn.loc.gov/2017014865

Manufactured in China

Photo credits: Cover Emile Signol/Getty Images; p. 5 © By permission of the British Library; p. 6 Amaia Arozena & Gotzon Iraloa/Moment/Getty Images; pp. 7, 15 De Agostini Picture Library/Getty Images; p. 10 Lior Mizrahi/ Getty Images; p. 12, 29 © Photos.com/Jupiterimages; p. 13, 36 Leemage/Corbis Historical/Getty Images; p. 17, 34, 40 © Photos.com/Thinkstock; p. 19 Photo 12/Universal Images Group/Getty Images; p. 21 Private Collection/ © Look and Learn/Bridgeman Images; p. 22 Christophel Fine Art/Universal Images Group /Getty Images; pp. 24–25 Dan Porges/Photolibrary/Getty Images; p. 27 © Staatliche Museen zu Berlin /Preussischer Kulturbesitz; p. 30 © semultura/Fotolia; p. 31 British Library, London, UK/ © British Library Board. All Rights Reserved/Bridgeman Images; p. 38 Hulton Archive/Getty Images; p. 41 Soltan Frédéric /Sygma/Getty Images; cover and interior pages background designs Mikado767/iStock/Thinkstock (circles), Andrey_Kuzmin/Shutterstock.com (forged metal).

CONTENTS

INTRODUCTION

From 1095 until the end of the Middle Ages, Christian warriors from Europe undertook a series of military campaigns, or Crusades, designed to take control of the Holy Land (the region of Palestine) back from the Muslims. After centuries of wars of expansion, Muslim powers had conquered some two-thirds of the ancient Christian world, including Palestine, Syria, Egypt, and Anatolia. Christian Crusading expeditions were also undertaken against Muslims in Spain, pagans in eastern Europe, and perceived enemies of the church in Christian Europe. Crusading decreased rapidly during the sixteenth century with the advent of the Protestant Reformation and the decline of papal authority.

Many Christians thought that by participating in the Crusades they would atone fully for their sins. On the breast of their tunics thousands of knights, soldiers, merchants, and peasants wore a cross of blood-red cloth to show they were going on Crusade. Those who returned wore the cross on their backs during the long voyage home. The Latin word for cross is *crux*, and from this word comes the words "crusade" and "crusader."

A Crusader, possibly King Henry III of England, giving homage. This thirteenth-century drawing, copied from the Westminster Psalter, c. 1200, depicts the armor typical of a Crusading knight and emphasizes the importance of military service to God and the church that all medieval knights would have felt.

Even though only the First and Third Crusades were successful in reclaiming parts of the Holy Land, the Crusades played an important role in the expansion of Europe. Historians have written about the excesses of the Crusades for centuries, and the Crusades remain today a fascinating yet controversial chapter in the history of Christianity, and in world history in general.

The Crusading movement was the result of a number of important factors. By the end of the eleventh century, the countries of Europe had become major powers. Western Europe was composed of several

Loarre Castle, located in the province of Huesca in the autonomous community of Aragon in Spain, is considered the best-preserved Romanesque fortress in Europe. It was built in the eleventh century on a promontory of limestone, giving it a great advantage against siege, as there was virtually no way to breach the castle from below.

kingdoms loosely describable as feudal. Their populations as well as their economies had grown dramatically, and their governments had become better organized, enabling European leaders to raise and command large armies. Such improvements in European society provided the necessary foundation upon which to build the Crusading movement.

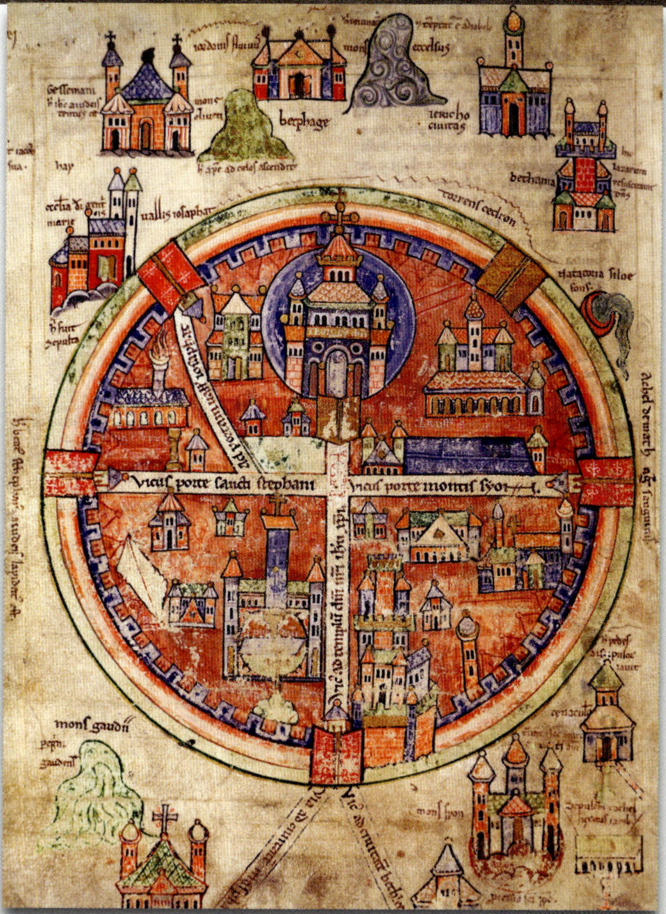

A thirteenth-century map of Jerusalem, with the cities of Gethsemane, Jericho, Bethany, and Hebron. This French miniature is part of Robert the Monk's *History of the First Crusade (Historia Hierosolymitana)*.

The nature of religious belief at the time was another important factor. According to the idea of holy war which took shape in the eleventh century, Christian warriors had a duty to do God's work by fighting for the church. The practice of pilgrimage to holy sites and the shrines of saints also influenced the Crusades. In the late eleventh century, a series of popes reorganized the church and exercised greater influence over Christians than had their predecessors.

These developments were affected by changes in the Holy Land and in the Byzantine Empire. In 1071 the Seljuq Turks defeated Byzantine armies at the battle of Manzikert and extended their control over much of Asia Minor. They persecuted Christians and attacked Christian holy places. They seized control of Jerusalem from the Muslim authority there. The previous rulers had allowed Christian pilgrims to visit the Holy City, but the Turks, who were recent converts to Islam, did not. Seljuq expansion southward continued, and in 1085 the capture of Antioch in Syria, one of the patriarchal sees of Christianity, was another blow to Byzantine prestige.

CHAPTER 1

WHAT LED TO THE CRUSADES?

Before the year 1000, most Christian pilgrims journeyed to the holy sites of Europe, including to the tombs of Saints Peter and Paul in Rome and to the city of Santiago de Compostela in northwestern Spain, where the tomb of Jesus' apostle Saint James was said to have been supernaturally revealed during the ninth century. The social effect of religious belief at the time was complex. Religion was moved by tales of signs and wonders, and it even attributed natural disasters to supernatural intervention.

JOURNEYS TO THE HOLY LAND

As a greater focus was given to the human Jesus and on the places associated with him, journeys to Jerusalem became increasingly popular. Some people believed that they were living at the end of time, and they thought it best to be in Jerusalem when Jesus

Sites of worship that were revered during the Crusades are still being preserved in the modern era. A $4 million restoration project within the rotunda of the Church of the Holy Sepulchre in Jerusalem was completed in early 2017. The church encloses the tomb in which Jesus was buried.

returned at the Last Judgment. Numerous expeditions were made to the Holy Land, where many Christian pilgrims visited the Holy Sepulchre, the tomb in Jerusalem in which Jesus was buried.

As the Seljuq Turks expanded their power in the eleventh century, the turmoil of these years disrupted normal political life and made the pilgrimage to Jerusalem difficult and often impossible. Stories of dangers and molestation reached the West and remained in the popular mind even after conditions improved. Furthermore, informed authorities began to realize that the power of the Muslim world now seriously menaced the West as well as the East. It was this realization that led to the Crusades.

HOLY LAND, HOLY WAR

Closely associated with the popular religious practice of pilgrimage was the Western concept of holy war. As the power of the Turks continued its spread in the East, Alexius I Comnenus, the Byzantine emperor, sent a plea for aid to Pope Urban II at Rome. The pope called a council at Clermont, France, in 1095. The Council of Clermont, where Urban II called for the First Crusade, renewed a movement known as the Peace of God that had been initiated by the medieval church to ensure peace and public order. It may seem contradictory that a council both promoted peace and officially sanctioned war, but the movement was designed to protect

Pope Urban II spoke to an assembly of Catholic followers at the Council of Clermont, 1095, in France, where he called for the First Crusade, asking them to go to war to rescue the Holy Land from the Turks.

those in distress; a driving factor of the First Crusade was to give aid to fellow Christians in the East. Tied to this was the idea that war to defend Christendom was not only justifiable, but a holy work and therefore pleasing to God.

Speaking with eloquence, Urban II urged his audience to undertake a Crusade to rescue the Holy Land. Fired with religious zeal, clergy, knights, and common people alike shouted, "God wills it!" And with that, Pope Urban's speech had inspired the First Crusade.

THE PEOPLE'S CRUSADE

Many people were so deeply stirred that they would not wait until the time set by the council for the First

ANTI-SEMITISM AND THE CRUSADES

Peter the Hermit's preaching in Germany inspired other groups of Crusaders, who also failed to reach Jerusalem. One of these groups was led by the notorious Count Emicho and was responsible for a series of pogroms, or massacres, of Jews in several Rhenish towns in 1096. Traditionally recognized as an important turning point in Jewish and Christian relations in the Middle Ages—in fact, it is often cited as a pivotal moment in the history of anti-Semitism—these attacks occurred first in Speyer and then with increasing ferocity in Worms, Mainz, and Cologne.

This French engraving by Lahure, 1866, is representative of the atrocities committed during the Rhineland massacres of the Jews that took place in 1096, during the People's Crusade.

(Continued on the next page)

(Continued from the previous page)

The Jews of these towns often sought, and sometimes received, the protection of the bishop or futilely took refuge in local homes and temples. Forced by the Crusaders to convert or die, many Jews chose death. There are accounts of Jews committing suicide and even killing their children rather than converting or submitting to execution by the Crusaders.

Though zealotry of this nature is not unique to Christianity, these massacres did not go unnoticed even by fellow Christians. Indeed, some contemporary Christian accounts attributed the defeat of the People's Crusade to them. After the massacres, the Crusaders moved on to Hungary, where they were routed by the Hungarian king and suffered heavy losses. Emicho, who may not have participated in all the pogroms, escaped and returned home in disgrace.

Crusade to begin. At least four separate bands started for the Holy Land early in 1096. One of them, a group of knights and peasants known as the People's Crusade, was led by Peter the Hermit and his associate, a knight named Walter Sansavoir. Peter was a brilliant preacher who caused thousands of people to join the Crusade. While his main body of followers was not well supplied and was a rather unruly group, they caused considerable disorder in Hungary and Bulgaria along the way.

This miniature dating to the fourteenth century in France depicts Peter the Hermit leading the People's Crusade to the Holy Land in 1096.

They managed to reach the capital of the Byzantine Empire in Constantinople (now Istanbul, Turkey), where Peter was able to request additional aid from Emperor Alexius I Comnenus. However, much of Peter's army, including Walter Sansavoir, was killed in an ambush by the Turks east of the city while they waited for their leader's return from the capital.

CHAPTER 2

THE FIRST CRUSADE: EMERGING ORDERS

In August 1096, the first real armies of knights and nobles began their march to Jerusalem. There were four main companies, led by Godfrey of Bouillon; Robert of Normandy; Raymond of Toulouse; and Bohemond, a Norman from southern Italy.

A BRUTAL WIN

The Crusaders went first to Constantinople, where their leaders met the Byzantine emperor and (unwillingly) swore an oath to restore imperial land to him. They then made a dangerous march across Asia Minor to Antioch. For seven months, they laid siege to the city, suffering almost as much as the people inside the city walls. After the Crusaders at last captured Antioch, they themselves were besieged by a Turkish army. In some three weeks, disease and famine killed many. The courage of the Crusaders faltered.

A band of Crusaders sets off for the Holy Land.

From there, the Crusaders' nearly hopeless situation changed in a strange way. A visionary, Peter Bartholomew, told the leaders of the Crusade that St. Andrew had revealed to him the location of the lance that had pierced Jesus' side. Many were skeptical, but

Peter found the spear. His discovery, real or feigned, and other heavenly visions fired the Crusaders with valor. They decided to fight the Turks outside the city and won a great victory. Many Crusaders believed that they were helped by an army of angels and the ghosts of dead Crusaders.

The Crusaders departed Antioch for Jerusalem in January 1099. A much-reduced Crusading army reached the Holy City on June 7, 1099. Undaunted, they besieged the well-supplied and well-fortified city. While the siege proceeded, a Muslim army set out from Egypt to attack the Crusaders. To assist their cause, the Crusaders made a religious procession around Jerusalem on July 8, 1099. The Crusaders finally took the city on July 15. Then they engaged in a shameful massacre of all the city's inhabitants, including civilian men, women, and children. After the slaughter, the Crusaders walked barefooted and bareheaded to kneel at the Holy Sepulchre. One week later, they defeated the army from Egypt.

A fair number of Crusaders returned home, but many stayed and were joined by new companies. Those who stayed chose Godfrey of Bouillon as ruler. They built castles and established Crusader states in the Holy Land. Special orders of knighthood, including the Knights Hospitallers, the Knights Templars, and, later, the Teutonic Knights, were created to protect the Holy Land.

After a month of siege, the Crusaders captured Jerusalem in 1099, effectively ending the First Crusade. This French illustration depicts the natives of Lorraine raising their standards, followed by the Flemish, natives of Champagne, and the Catalans.

MILITARY TRAINING, MONASTIC VOWS

The first of the three great European military and religious orders to arise were the Knights of the Hospital of St. John, or the Hospitallers. Formed in the late 1000s to provide medical care for sick and wounded Christian pilgrims in the region of Palestine, the order took on military functions starting in the early 1100s. The Knights Templars was formed in about 1119 to provide military protection for the pilgrims. Its name came from the location of its headquarters in the former Temple of Solomon in Jerusalem. The Teutonic Knights, or Teutonic Order, was a German order founded in 1189–90 and modeled on the Hospitallers.

The members of these orders conformed to both military and religious discipline. They were soldiers with the obligations and training of knighthood, but they took monastic vows. They fought in the Crusades, established castles, garrisons, and hospitals in Palestine, and formed branches in their home countries. In time, kings and others presented the orders with power and possessions in many lands, and they became important factors in European history. Their leaders were summoned to the great church councils. Their houses were used as strongholds for the royal treasure. Kings, when pressed for money, depended upon them for loans.

Zur Geschichte der Kostüme.

Dreiundvierzigster Bogen.

XII. und XIII. Jahrhundert.

Johanniterinnen.

Johanniter.

Hofmeiste

ichener B

8. Aufl

Alle Rechte vor

er in

Members of the Crusading orders are shown in costume, dating to the twelfth and thirteenth centuries. Clockwise from the top left, the Hospitaller Sisters, Knights Hospitallers, Knights Templars, and Teutonic Knights are represented.

THE KNIGHTS TEMPLARS

At the beginning of the religious military order of knighthood known as the Knights Templars, the group consisted of eight or nine French knights who devoted themselves to protecting Christians on pilgrimage to Jerusalem. The knights were given quarters near the site of the former Temple of Jerusalem, from which they derived their name. Taking vows of poverty and chastity, they performed courageous service, and their numbers increased rapidly, partly because of the propagandistic writing of St. Bernard de Clairvaux. They flourished for two centuries, expanding to other countries, growing in number to twenty thousand, and acquiring vast wealth and property. By 1304 false rumors of irreligious practices and

An engraving of the last grand master of the Knights Templars, Jacques de Molay (1243–1314), in the robes of his order.

blasphemies—including idol worship and worship of a cat—had made them the target of persecution. In 1307 Philip IV of France and Pope Clement V initiated the offensive that culminated in the Templars' final suppression in 1312, including the confiscation of all their property and the imprisonment or execution of many members. Their last leader, Jacques de Molay (1243–1314), was judged a relapsed heretic and burned at the stake.

After its demise, the order became an object of myth and legend. The Templars were associated with the Holy Grail and were identified as defenders of the Grail castle throughout the remainder of the Middle Ages. In the eighteenth century, the Freemasons claimed to have received esoteric knowledge from the Templars. Some contemporary authors, writing what most scholars regard as fantasy, have continued to involve the Templars in a variety of conspiracy theories.

LATER HISTORY OF THE ORDERS

The wealth of the Templars appears to have been one reason why Philip IV of France and Pope Clement V suppressed the order and took its property in the early 1300s. Many of the order's members were imprisoned, tortured, or executed on false charges of immorality and blasphemy.

In the 1300s, the Hospitallers established themselves on the island of Rhodes, which they ruled as an independent state until it fell to the Turks in 1523. Charles V, emperor of the Holy Roman Empire, gave

The Knights Hospitallers contributed quite a bit to the island of Rhodes in their two-hundred-year rule there, including the fortification of the Old City. They built up the Palace of the Grand Master, a wall, a moat, a bridge, and other protections against besieging enemies.

them the island of Malta, and they came to be known as the Knights of Malta. Napoleon forced them off Malta in 1798. Today, they are headquartered in Rome and operate in most parts of the world.

The Teutonic Knights renewed their Crusading activities in the fourteenth and fifteenth centuries by warring against pagans in eastern Europe. They combined colonizing and trading with their ingrained religious zeal, and had much to do with the founding of Prussia. At the time of the Protestant Reformation in 1525, the order was dissolved in Prussia due to its Roman Catholic nature, but survived in other parts of Europe. Napoleon dissolved the entire order in 1809, but in 1834 the Austrian emperor refounded it as a charitable religious order with headquarters in Vienna.

CHAPTER 3

THE ERA OF THE SECOND AND THIRD CRUSADES

The loss of the important Crusader city Edessa and the renewed spread of Muslim power in Asia Minor inspired the Second Crusade (1147–49). It had long been apparent that Edessa was vulnerable, but its loss came as a shock to Eastern and Western Christians. Urgent pleas for aid soon reached Europe, and in 1145 Pope Eugenius III issued a formal Crusade bull. It was the first of its kind, with precisely worded provisions designed to protect Crusaders' families and property and reflecting contemporary advances in canon law.

KINGS TAKE ARMS

Unlike the First Crusade, the Second was led by Europe's greatest rulers, Emperor Conrad III of Germany and King Louis VII of France, joined by his wife, Eleanor of Aquitaine. The Second Crusade

ST. BERNARD OF CLAIRVAUX

The preaching of St. Bernard of Clairvaux in France and Germany inspired many to take up the cross for the Second Crusade. Bernard revolutionized Crusade ideology, asserting that the Crusade was not merely an act of charity or a war to secure the holy places but a means of redemption. In St. Bernard's view, Christ, in his mercy, was offering the warriors of Europe a blessed avenue of salvation, a means by which they could give up all they had to follow him.

It has been said that Emperor Conrad, reluctant to take up arms, was won over by the eloquence of St. Bernard. The Knights Templars, a monastic-military organization dedicated to protecting pilgrims on their way to Jerusalem, also turned to St. Bernard to compose their rule and eulogy, which was officially sanctioned by the Council of Troyes in 1128.

An altarpiece from the sixteenth century depicts St. Bernard of Clairvaux, an influential monk whose preaching inspired many people to go on the Second Crusade. St. Bernard asserted that the Crusade was not merely an act of charity or a war to take back the holy places but a means for people to secure redemption.

(Continued on the next page)

(Continued from the previous page)

Searching for an explanation for the collapse of the Second Crusade, St. Bernard turned to Scripture. He preached that the Crusade failed because of the sinfulness of Europe. Only through the purification and prayers of Christian men and women would God relent and bestow victory on his knights once more. This belief became central to Crusading ideology and an important impetus for movements of lay piety during the Middle Ages.

also differed from its predecessor in that there were three objectives rather than one. While the kings of Germany and France marched east to restore Edessa, other Crusaders went to Spain to fight Muslims or to the shores of the Baltic Sea to fight the pagan Wends.

The situation in the East had also changed. Manuel Comnenus, the Byzantine emperor, was not pleased to discover another Crusade headed toward Constantinople. The Second Crusade wreaked havoc on his foreign policy, which included an alliance with Germany, Venice, and the pope against the Normans. It also complicated the emperor's peaceful relationship with the Turkish sultan. Manuel made a truce with the sultan in 1146 to make certain that the Crusade would not cause the sultan to attack Byzantine lands in Asia.

Emperor Conrad left Germany in May 1147, accompanied by his fellow noblemen, the kings of Poland and Bohemia, and his nephew Frederick (the future emperor Frederick I). Upon arrival in September, Conrad's poorly disciplined troops created tension in Constantinople. Rejecting Manuel Comnenus's advice, Conrad moved his force directly toward Anatolia. After being set upon by the Turks and almost destroyed, Conrad and his few survivors retreated to Nicaea.

This late-fourteenth-century drawing from *Les Chroniques de Saint-Denis* is divided into two scenes. In the left, Eleanor of Aquitaine marries Louis VII in 1137; in the right, Louis VII departs on the Second Crusade (1147).

King Louis and Eleanor followed the land route from France across Europe and arrived at Constantinople in October, a month after the Germans. From there, he and Conrad started along the coastal route to Ephesus—but the German emperor had to return to Constantinople due to illness. The French passage from Ephesus to Antioch in midwinter was extremely harrowing. Supplies ran short, and the Byzantines were unjustly blamed. Manuel defended his cities against the angry Crusaders, which meant that the French spent more energy fighting Christians than Muslims.

The Crusade's original goal of recapturing Edessa was no longer feasible.

Once Louis and Conrad reached Jerusalem, many French and German notables assembled with Queen Melisende, her son Baldwin III (who at the time was coruler with his mother of the Crusader state of Jerusalem), and the barons to discuss how best to proceed. Despite earlier losses, they were able to rally an army of nearly fifty thousand men to attack Damascus. The attack soon failed, however. The Second Crusade had become a disaster. The entire venture was poorly managed, worsening relations between the Crusaders and the Byzantine Empire and encouraging Muslim leaders Unur and Nur al-Din.

The Umayyad Mosque, also known as the Great Mosque of Damascus, is located in the Old City of Damascus, Syria. It was commissioned in 705 and completed in 715 CE, and has remained a focal point for the city despite political and imperial changes throughout the centuries.

OUTREMER: THE CRUSADER STATES

Outremer—French for "overseas"—was the general name used for the Crusader states of Edessa, Antioch, Tripoli, and Jerusalem after victories in the First Crusade. By the 1170s, these areas of Latin settlement had developed well-established governments largely made up of Frankish residents who had learned to adjust to the new environment and were concerned with administration. A few were fluent in Arabic; others knew enough of the language to communicate with local inhabitants.

In fundamentals, they were still Latin Chris-

A psalter for Queen Melisende dating to the twelfth century may have been created in Constantinople. The manuscript shows certain Byzantine characteristics, but it has also been done in the tradition of French art—as in this example of the Virgin surrounded by apostles and Christ holding her soul, and two angels above.

(Continued on the next page)

(Continued from the previous page)

tians who adhered to the traditions of their French forebears. All documents, such as the Assizes of the Court of the Bourgeois, were drawn up in French or Latin. However, many Franks adopted native dress, ate native food, employed native physicians, and married Syrian, Armenian, or converted Muslim women.

Artists and architects were influenced by Byzantine and Arab craftsmen. Castles followed Byzantine models and were often built on the old foundations, though Western ideas were also incorporated. New churches were built or additions made to existing structures, as, for example, the Church of the Holy Sepulchre, in the Romanesque style of the homeland.

All in all, the Franks developed a distinctive culture and achieved a sense of identity. Until quarrels between barons weakened the monarchy in later years, the Latin kingdom showed remarkable vitality and ingenuity. It was one of the more sophisticated governmental achievements of the Middle Ages.

THE POWER OF SALADIN

For the next several decades, the Crusader states enjoyed relative stability. However, in the 1180s the situation worsened, both due to internal problems and the rise of a new Muslim leader, Saladin. In 1187 he won two great victories against the Crusaders. In July, he wiped out a Crusader army at the Battle of Hattin in northern Palestine and executed two hundred Knights Hospitallers and Knights Templars who had survived the battle. In October, he seized Jerusalem. But unlike the Crusaders in 1099, he did not slay his defeated foes; he permitted many to go free, some even without ransom.

Saladin's conquest inspired the Third Crusade (1189–91). The leaders were Richard the Lion-Hearted of England; Philip Augustus of France; and the powerful emperor of Germany, Frederick I, or Frederick Barbarossa, so called because of his red beard.

Although excommunicated by Pope Alexander III and a supporter of antipopes in the 1160s and '70s, Frederick had made peace with the church in 1177 and for some time had genuinely wanted to go on Crusade again. But the German expedition collapsed when Frederick—now nearly seventy years old and approaching the end of an eventful career—drowned while trying to ford a mountain stream in Asia Minor in June 1190. His death broke the morale of the German army, and only a small remnant pushed forward. To Saladin and the Muslims, who had been seriously alarmed by Frederick's approach, the emperor's death seemed an act of God.

Richard and Philip took their armies by sea, sailing from the French Mediterranean coast. When they reached the Holy Land, they joined the Christians besieging Acre. After a siege of twenty-three months, Acre fell in July 1191. After quarreling with Richard, Philip returned to France. Richard stayed, recapturing several cities and arranging a three-year

Richard the Lion-Hearted of England leads his soldiers during the Third Crusade.

truce with Saladin in 1192 that permitted pilgrims to visit the holy sites. The Third Crusade failed to attain its main objective, the retaking of Jerusalem, but in every other way it was considered a success.

CHAPTER 4

CRUSADES OF THE THIRTEENTH CENTURY

In 1198, the new pope, Innocent III, proclaimed a new Crusade, and four years later it was launched. The Fourth Crusade (1202–04) was aimed at Egypt, because the general opinion at the time was that the Holy Land could only be protected by attacking Muslim power centers.

THE FOURTH CRUSADE

In preparation for the Fourth Crusade, France commissioned the Venetians to provide the fleet of ships the Crusaders would use to cross the Mediterranean Sea. But fewer Crusaders than expected arrived, and they could not raise the amount of money promised to the Venetians. Doge Enrico Dandolo, leader of Venice, said the Crusaders could still have ships if they would help him capture the rival commercial city of Zara. Even though it was a Christian city, the Crusaders seized it in November 1202.

This miniature of the conquest of Constantinople by the Crusaders during the Fourth Crusade (1202–04) dates back to the fifteenth century. The image shows their arrival by sea, via the Mediterranean.

Afterward, Prince Alexius, a rival to the throne of Byzantium, offered to assist the Crusaders if they helped overthrow the emperor there. They did so, and Alexius became emperor. When he could not uphold his end of the bargain, however, the Crusaders seized Constantinople. They pillaged the magnificent city and divided the emperor's lands before setting up the Latin Empire of Constantinople (1204–61). The Byzantines eventually regained control of their empire, but they remained seriously weakened by the Crusaders' conquest.

A FINAL PUSH

In the thirteenth century, Crusades were launched against new enemies of the Christian church. Pope Innocent III approved the Albigensian Crusade against heretics in southern France. Northern French knights helped suppress heresy in the south and restored the king's control of that region. The Teutonic Knights began to shift their Crusading efforts from the Holy Lands to eastern Europe, where they fought pagans and converted them to Christianity. The pope also used the Crusade to undermine his political rivals in the Holy Roman Empire.

Crusades to the East also continued in the thirteenth century. The Fifth Crusade (1218–21) took place in Egypt and failed because of disagreements among its leaders. The Crusade of Emperor Frederick II (1228–29) differed from all the other Crusades in two ways: the pope had excommunicated the emperor rather than supported him, and Frederick freed Jerusalem by peaceful negotiation instead of military conquest. In 1244 the Turks seized Jerusalem. This led to the first (1249) of two Crusades headed by Louis IX of France. The Crusaders tried to take Egypt as the western key to Palestine, but Louis was captured and forced to pay a "king's ransom." Further Muslim successes against the Crusaders inspired Louis' second Crusade (1270). Louis died of plague shortly after he landed in North Africa, and the Crusade failed.

THE CHILDREN'S CRUSADE

The Children's Crusade actually involved many kinds of people, including the elderly, women, and the poor alongside young adults and children. In 1212, the religious enthusiasm that had led knights to go on Crusade also touched the common people, who lacked the wealth or training to fight a war on their own. An odd collective spirit emerged in France and Germany without papal motivation or approval, revealing that many in the Middle Ages were independently inspired by the idea of rescuing the Holy Land.

The French phase of the Children's Crusade was led by Stephen, a shepherd boy from an area near Cloyes. In the spring of 1212 he said that Jesus had appeared to him in a vision and given him a letter for King Philip Augustus of France (presumably encouraging the king to go on Crusade again). Stephen led his large band of followers to Paris to deliver the letter. The king graciously received Stephen and then ordered him and his followers to return home.

This drawing depicts a group of children known as the Cockhorse Regiment who took part in the Children's Crusade of 1212. While the Children's Crusade actually involved many different types of people, it is startling to see such young people taking up arms for the cause.

News of Stephen's preaching spread into Germany. It inspired the young man Nicholas of Cologne to band German children and others together to free the Holy Land. He believed that God would open up the Mediterranean Sea to allow them to walk there. Nicholas led his many followers over the Alps into Italy. They reached Genoa, where the sea did not part. Some of them then went to Rome, where Pope Innocent III gently ordered them home. Few ever reached their homes in Germany. Some accounts indicate that merchants sold many of the children into slavery; it is also likely that many found jobs in Italy.

In 1291 the Muslims took Acre, the last Crusader stronghold, and the Crusaders were finally expelled from the Middle East. Despite this loss and the failures of the earlier Crusades, the ideal of Crusading remained important. Crusades were called to protect Constantinople and southeastern Europe in the fifteenth century, though these efforts ultimately failed. The Christian reconquest of Spain that had begun in the eleventh century ended successfully in 1492 when Granada, the last Muslim outpost in Spain, fell to Christian knights.

RESULTS OF THE CRUSADES

The Crusades formed an important part of the transformation of European society in the twelfth and thirteenth centuries. They were part of the expansion

An illustration from the thirteenth-century encyclopedia *Speculum Majus* (Great Mirror) harks back to the Third Crusade, depicting the Siege of Acre (1191), when the Crusaders conquered this stronghold in the Middle East. The Crusaders were finally expelled from the region when they lost Acre to Mamluk forces in 1291.

of Europe and laid the foundation for the Age of Discovery. The Crusades also introduced new ideas and goods to Europe.

By the late eleventh century, the population of Europe had grown significantly. Over the next two centuries, large numbers of people would need to find more living space across Europe and into the Middle East. The Crusades opened up trade contact with the East, and new foods and textiles began to appear in the markets and fairs of Europe. The new products included spices, cane sugar, buckwheat, rice, apricots, watermelons, oranges, limes, lemons, cotton, damask, satin, velvet, and dyestuffs. Europeans also learned the art of papermaking from Muslims.

In its own way, the Crusades introduced western Europe to the great civilizations of the Islamic and

An aerial view of the Krak des Chevaliers (Castle of the Knights), located in Syria. Constructed in the twelfth century by the Knights Hospitallers, it is known as the greatest fortress built by European Crusaders in the Middle East and one of the most notable surviving examples of medieval military architecture.

Byzantine worlds—though often over the bloody arena of war. The reconquest of Spain brought Arabic science and philosophy to Western Christians. Crusades to the East exposed Europeans to the great cities and culture of Islam—including new forms of castle building—and contact with the Byzantine Empire provided access to ancient Greek learning. The Fourth Crusade, however, did serious damage to relations between the Roman Catholic and Eastern Orthodox churches.

The Crusades were a factor in Europe's development during the twelfth and thirteenth centuries, but generalizations must be made with caution. Loss of life on all sides was considerable, and the Crusaders ultimately failed to regain the Holy Land. The Crusades did succeed in creating new religious orders and shaping religious practices in Europe. They also prepared the way for a later wave of European expansion in the fifteenth and sixteenth centuries and the European discovery of the New World.

GLOSSARY

anti-Semitism Hostility toward or discrimination against Jews as a religious, ethnic, or racial group.

bull A solemn papal letter sealed with a bulla or with a red-ink imprint of the device on the bulla; an edict or decree.

Crusade Any of the military expeditions undertaken by Christian powers in the eleventh, twelfth, and thirteenth centuries to win the Holy Land from the Muslims.

ecclesiastical Of or relating to a church, especially as an established institution.

eloquence The art or power of speaking or writing in a forceful and convincing way.

esoteric Requiring knowledge that is restricted to a small group; designed to be understood by the specially initiated.

eulogy A commendatory oration or writing; high praise.

feudal Of, relating to, or having the characteristics of a medieval estate in land granted by a lord on condition of homage or service.

heresy Adherence to a religious opinion contrary to church doctrine.

Holy See The ecclesiastical jurisdiction of the Catholic Church in Rome.

monastic Of or relating to monasteries or monks.

pagan A follower of a polytheistic religion (as in ancient Rome).

papal Of or relating to a pope or to the Roman Catholic Church.

patriarchy Social organization marked by the supremacy of the father in the clan or family, the legal dependence of wives and children, and the carrying of descent and inheritance through the male line.

pogrom An organized massacre of helpless people, usually because of their race or religion.

psalter A collection of Psalms for liturgical or devotional use.

salvation Deliverance from the power and effects of sin.

sanction A formal decree; especially, an ecclesiastical decree.

sepulchre A place of burial; tomb.

siege A military blockade of a city or fortified place to compel it to surrender.

valor Strength of mind or spirit that enables a person to encounter danger with firmness; bravery.

FOR FURTHER READING

Abbott, Jacob. *The Story of Richard the Lionheart*. San Diego, CA: Didactic Press, 2013.

Edgington, Susan. *The First Crusade: The Capture of Jerusalem in AD 1099* (Library of the Middle Ages). New York, NY: Rosen Publishing, 2003.

Geyer, Flora. *Saladin: The Warrior Who Defended His People*. National Geographic, 2006.

Harpur, James. *The Crusades* (Prime Time History). New York, NY: Rosen Publishing, 2008.

Hilliam, David. *Richard the Lionheart and the Third Crusade: The English King Confronts Saladin, AD 1191* (The Library of the Middle Ages). New York, NY: Rosen Publishing, 2004.

Hoggard, Brian. *Crusader Castles: Christian Fortresses in the Middle East* (The Library of the Middle Ages). New York, NY: Rosen Publishing, 2004.

Jeffrey, Gary. *Crusades* (Graphic Medieval History). New York, NY: Crabtree Publishing, 2014.

Rice Jr., Earle. *Eleanor of Aquitaine* (Biography from Ancient Civilizations). Hallandale, FL: Mitchell Lane Publishers, 2009.

Riley, Michael, and Jamie Byrom. *The Crusades*. London, UK: Hodder Education, 2013.

Talib, Qaiser M. *Salah Ad-Din and the Crusades*. London, UK: Ta-Ha Publishers, 2012.

WEBSITES

Because of the changing nature of internet links, Rosen Publishing has developed an online list of websites related to the subject of this book. This site is updated regularly. Please use this link to access this list:

http://www.rosenlinks.com/EIMA/Crusades

INDEX